Praise for
Prayer

"Moments of prayer, meditation, and quiet seem rarer than ever before in these days of constant distraction, busyness, and noise. Finding those moments is difficult but necessary for our flourishing as humans. This simple but profound book has been one of our favorite tools in our search for God in the midst."

—JAY AND KATHERINE WOLF, coauthors and cofounders of *Hope Heals*

"Just one page of *Prayer* could change your life. Deep, beautiful, and centered, this book drives us ever closer to being people who love God and love each other. Justin's reflections show evidence of someone who has spent a lot of time journeying with Jesus, and Scott's illustrations are worthy of meditation. This book has helped me move deeper into the presence of God."

—MATT MIKALATOS, author of *Good News for a Change*

"Justin and Scott have compiled the most beautiful anthology of prayers and images, interwoven with suggestions for contemplation and spiritual practices. I've been using these words and pictures in my own devotional life for a couple of years. They have refreshed and renewed me. This book is a gift."

—MICHAEL FROST, author of *Surprise the World* and *Keep Christianity Weird*

"McRoberts and Erickson are flip artists: they take what is commonly assumed or known and flip it in unexpected ways, all for the sake of greater authenticity and deeper wisdom. Their book *Prayer* surprises, interrupts, explodes, confronts, and inspires. I encourage you to take up their invitation for *Forty Days of Practice*."

—MARK LABBERTON, president of Fuller Theological Seminary

"*Prayer* by Justin McRoberts and Scott Erickson is a gift of a book. Its compelling prayers and captivating images resonated deep in my soul. Sacred in its sincerity and simplicity, *Prayer* is a forty-day path we can walk together to live out the spiritual truths that make ourselves—and our world—uncompromisingly whole."
—SARAH THEBARGE, author of *The Invisible Girls* and *Well*

"In my home we have a special shelf where we keep sacred things of beauty. On the shelf are a few icons, seashells, the Book of Common Prayer, and this book, *Prayer.* Each person in my family—from children to adults—sits in quiet wonder as they flip these pages. This meditative and practical book brings together prayer, practices, and visual art to provide a feast for the soul. McRoberts and Erickson have created something beautiful, thoughtful, and mesmerizing."
—TISH HARRISON WARREN, priest in the Anglican Church in North America and author of *Liturgy of the Ordinary*

"With compelling art and thoughtful prose, this little book, *Prayer,* delivers big inspiration. In addition to personal stories and practical advice, Scott and Justin offer us a fresh path into daily contemplation that is as simple as it is meaningful. I already know I'll be coming back to these pages again and again."
—JAMIE WRIGHT, author of *The Very Worst Missionary*

"My friends Justin McRoberts and Scott Erickson have prompted us to seek God with our whole selves in their book *Prayer.* I'm grateful for this invitation to prayer and urge others to accept it as well!"
—MICHAEL WEAR, author of *Reclaiming Hope*

"Prayer empowers us to walk by faith and not by sight. In a world where death, oppression, and violence all too often feel like the final words, we're prone to forget that prayer truly changes things. Prayer begets revelation, enabling us to see, name, and confess the brokenness within us and our world. Prayer then leads to repentance, which reorients our posture toward God and neighbor. This book prophetically uses art to inspire us to remember God's faithfulness amid the darkness. It also structures prayer in ways that draw us simultaneously inward and outward, producing a more faithful witness."

—DOMINIQUE DUBOIS GILLIARD, author of *Rethinking Incarceration*

"Scott and Justin's book *Prayer* made it to the place of highest honor in our home: the bathroom throne. This is not a book you devour. It's a book you savor. Each page contains a treasure . . . like chocolate truffles for the soul."

—SHANE CLAIBORNE, activist and author of *Beating Guns*

"*Prayer* is beautiful, reflective, and powerfully affecting. What Justin McRoberts and Scott Erickson have given us is not simply a book about prayer but rather an invitation to commune with the divine. Using art and words, they offer our minds and hearts fresh thoughts and themes to meditate on, to utter, to believe. This book is an experience, one that will inspire your imagination not just to connect with God but to engage the Creator as the creative being that you are."

—MATTHEW PAUL TURNER, author of *When God Made You* and *When I Pray for You*

PRAYER

Forty Days of Practice

JUSTIN McROBERTS
& SCOTT ERICKSON

WATERBROOK

PRAYER

Hardcover ISBN 978-0-525-65305-9
eBook ISBN 978-0-525-65306-6

Published in the United States by WaterBrook, an imprint of the Crown Publishing Group, a division of Penguin Random House LLC, New York.

WATERBROOK® and its deer colophon are registered trademarks of Penguin Random House LLC.

Library of Congress Cataloging-in-Publication Data
Names: McRoberts, Justin, author.
Title: Prayer : forty days of practice / Justin McRoberts, Scott Erickson.
Description: First Edition. | Colorado Springs : WaterBrook, 2019.
Identifiers: LCCN 2018023917 | ISBN 9780525653059 (hardcover) | ISBN 9780525653066 (electronic)
Subjects: LCSH: Prayer—Christianity.
Classification: LCC BV215 .M388 2019 | DDC 248.3/2—dc23
LC record available at https://lccn.loc.gov/2018023917

Printed in the United States of America
2021

10 9

SPECIAL SALES
Most WaterBrook books are available at special quantity discounts when purchased in bulk by corporations, organizations, and special-interest groups. Custom imprinting or excerpting can also be done to fit special needs. For information, please e-mail specialmarketscms@penguinrandomhouse.com or call 1-800-603-7051.

In this field there lies a hidden treasure, if only I could find it and dig it up.

—Hans Urs von Balthasar, *Prayer*

BEFORE YOU BEGIN

Creators of all kinds (particularly authors) tend to refer to our work as "content." I've come to think that's a bit of a misnomer. I'd like to suggest that Scott and I make resources and tools that stir, inform, and inspire human lives, but that it is what is happening in those human lives that is most rightly understood as content. In that spirit, this book is rooted in the content of two human lives (Scott's and mine) but should not be, as an artifact, most accurately considered content.

This book is a piece of art.
This book is an act of love.
This book is a redemptive tool.
This book is a resource.
This book is designed to stir, inform, and inspire you.
This book is not "content."
The ongoing conversation between you and God is content.

— —— — —

I remember kneeling next to my mother's bed, trying to balance a small porcelain statue of Jesus on the lumpy bedspread. When I thought I had set it firmly upright, I folded my hands and closed my eyes to pray, only to be interrupted by the light thump of Jesus toppling over again. I don't know how many times I repeated the process, but as best as I remember, I never got around to the actual business of praying because I couldn't set up correctly.

As I have with so much else in my process of faith, I had allowed mechanics to trump essence. I thought I needed all the right elements properly executed in order to pray. Instead of seeing those elements as helpful (which they most certainly can be), I treated them as essential (which they most certainly are not). I was like a man who had seen water delivered only in clear glasses and would not, regardless of how deep his thirst, drink from another container. I think you will agree that the method of delivery, be it glass or plastic or the cupped shape of a human hand, can be very helpful and might even be beautiful, but it is the act of drinking that matters first.

I have come to believe that allowing the mechanics of prayer to trump essence presents a grave danger. Having grown distracted or disillusioned by mechanics, I might too easily abandon something I essentially need. You see, I believe I pray because I am human rather than because I am religious. An essential aspect of my nature points me beyond my nature and, I further believe, beyond what I know of nature altogether. Some primal thing urges me to search for and connect with the Divine. Tradition can and does provide language, shape, and space for that primal urge to pray, but the instinct to connect with God does not emanate from that tradition. Having allowed the mechanics of tradition to take a back seat to the essential nature of prayer, I can more readily receive the language and imagery of tradition as a great gift.

Our desire in this book is to extend a gift to you from our own practices and traditions by providing language and imagery you may find helpful for your practice of prayer. Herein, you will find us doing that in four ways:

- Guided prayers
- Contemplative imagery
- Meditations
- Suggested practices

Guided Prayers

Since 1998, as a writer of both prose and song, I have worked to provide language for the process of faith and life. In a sense, I am offering back a gift given to me. I have often needed the words of others to help me see what was in my soul when my own language failed me.

From Thomas Merton to Dr. Martin Luther King Jr. and from my neighbor to immediate family, the gift of others' words has been like borrowing a cup from someone else so that I could pour my life into it . . . or pour it out.

May the language herein be that same kind of gift to you. Consider focusing on one guided prayer (and its corresponding image) each day and see what you find in you.

Contemplative Imagery

Scott and I wanted to create something that invites you to do far more than simply read what is written and agree or disagree. The design of this book is an invitation to stop, listen, hear, see, recognize, and contemplate your life, the lives of those you love, and the presence of God in, through, and around all of it. That kind of contemplation takes what Scott likes to call an "excavation of the soul"—the kind of digging that good art invites us to do.

In Scott's words:

> We've all read a book that has pictures in it. Most likely the illustrations creatively visualized the words being communicated in the story. If it was a children's book, the images did all the heavy lifting in keeping your attention. That's how most of us experience imagery.
>
> But I don't think that's what these images are for. I think imagery is another language entirely. Neuroscientist Dr. Andrew Newberg agrees, writing in his book *How God Changes Your Brain,* "Drawing is a form of communication that is neurologically distinct from writing and speech. . . . In essence, words and pictures are two integrated elements of language, and most words . . . have an 'image' quality associated with them. If the right hemisphere is injured, words and

pictures lose their meaning." He continues, "Words are not enough to describe a spiritual experience."*

Prayer is a conversation about everything. Words and images are vital tools that can help us grow in this endless and ongoing conversation, but we must understand that the words and images we use are not the content itself. They are excavation tools that help dig toward and into the real content: the ongoing, ever-present conversation between us and the Divine.

* Andrew Newberg and Mark Robert Waldman, *How God Changes Your Brain: Breakthrough Findings from a Leading Neuroscientist* (New York: Ballantine, 2009), 99–100.

Scott has often been asked what his paintings mean. And while questions of intrinsic meaning can lead to interesting conversations, perhaps a better question about visual art is, What does the piece draw out of you? Henri Nouwen's remarkable book *The Return of the Prodigal Son* is a retelling of his interactions with Rembrandt's iconic work by that same name. Rather than centering the book on what can be found in the painting, Nouwen shares the ways Rembrandt's work dug into and unearthed pieces of his soul, helping him see things in himself in need of repair, as well as things healed and in the process of restoration.

May the imagery herein be that same kind of gift to you.

Meditations

The transitions between the book's sections are highlighted by meditations on the essence or nature of prayer. By calling them meditations instead of essays or even reflections, we are inviting you to engage with them a touch differently. Rather than asking yourself, *What do I think about this?* or *Is this correct?* pay attention to your responses, emotions, and thoughts. What is happening in you as you read through the meditations? In other words, we're not asking you to come to a conclusion or make a judgment about the content or agree with the philosophical or theological angle taken. These meditations, much like the brief prayers and images, are intended to stir what is in you rather than get information into you.

Suggested Practices

Each of the six meditations is paired with a way to practice the discipline of prayer. Our desire is to be a help to you in your long-term process rather than provide a singular moment of inspiration. Including these suggested practices is a way for us to offer something you can return to and use on the road ahead, kind of like a book you'd keep with you in your bag or on your nightstand.

We suggest allowing yourself some time to practice unfamiliar types of prayer. Not everything works for everyone, but we've found that it can take a fair bit of work and honest trial for people to discover what truly works for them. For both Scott and me, engaging the almost endless variety of methods and shapes of prayer has been a freeing and soul-shaping gift. May the practices suggested herein (journaling, exercise, fasting, meditation, lament, and intercession) be that same kind of gift for you.

— —— — —

May I . . . Make an Assumption?

In putting this book together, Scott and I assume the loving and redemptive activity of the Divine in, around, and through your life. In that light, framing our prayers with "May I . . ." is a way to enter into the extant movement of God rather than feel we are responsible for chasing Him down somewhere we aren't yet living.

The "May I . . ." language of these prayers borrows from the jussive mood in the Genesis creation account, wherein God speaks all things into being by saying, "Let there be . . ." The jussive mood suggests that Reality should be the way God desires it, not simply because He says so but because being shaped and ordered according to the Divine Will is the fullest expression of Reality. Praying "May I . . ." is a way to enter into the work God is already doing in, around, and through us, according to His Will and design.

We join the mother of Jesus, Mary, who prayed, "May Your word be fulfilled in me," or "May it be with me as You say," or "Let it be with me according to Your word," or "May everything You have said about me come true." Praying "May I . . ." means leaning into what God is doing and how the Divine Will has set things in and around us in motion.

Teach Me to Number My Days

While there is a great deal of value in prayer guides offering a more structured and chronologically ordered approach to the practice, we're offering something rather different here. Consider the layout and format of this book an invitation to let your soul, rather than a page number or calendar day, tell you where to stay or move and when. Certainly, you are welcome to start with the first prayer and work straight through to prayer 40 in linear fashion (the book's layout allows for that as well). But should you find yourself resonating with a particular prayer, stay there. And if you land on a prayer that just doesn't connect with or stir anything in you, feel free to move on.

Because it isn't the format of this book that matters most.

Nor is it the words in this book.

Nor its imagery.

What's happening in you is what matters.

What's happening in you is real content.

—Justin McRoberts

*May love be stronger in me
than the fear of the pain
That comes with caring.*

May I cease to be annoyed that others
are not as I wish they were,
Since I am not as I wish I was.

May I have vision and courage
to join God in the places
He's already working
rather than feel
Responsible for bringing Him
with me.

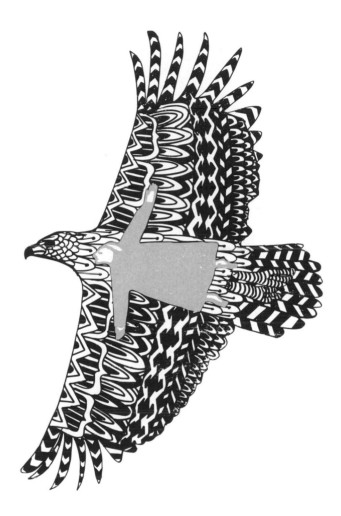

*May the reality that I cannot know
the whole truth
Never keep me from bearing witness
to what I can and do see.*

May I have the courage to believe that everything I do matters.

AGAIN AROUND THE LABYRINTH

The prayer labyrinth featured three circles of stone steps pressed into the grass, initially by the hands of its builders and then over time by the feet of visitors like me. Entering the first circle, I tried to quiet my mind and pray. But even as I concentrated on my footsteps, my mind turned to worries about work: things unfinished and things forgotten. Distracted and frustrated, I chased those thoughts away as best I could, but all throughout the first circle, work filled my mind.

I shook off my disappointment and entered the second circle, committed to silencing my inner person and to praying. Predictably, my mind wandered again, turning to future plans: things I was working on, things I wanted to do, and things I was inspired by. Once more I chased those thoughts away, shaking them out of my head as best I could. I ended the second circle feeling somewhat defeated.

I waited until my pulse slowed, took several deep breaths, and with a new resolve began slowly walking the third circle. This time my mind buzzed with the noise of relational strife: broken friendships and distances filled with miscommunication or misunderstanding. I slowed my steps again, having noticed that my pace had quickened with my heartbeat. I stopped, tilting my head back and sighing toward the sky in frustration. Looking down, I saw I had only three stone steps from the end of the third circle to the center of the labyrinth.

I stepped on each stone, saying, "I'm so sorry. I can't focus."

Finally, I stood in the middle of the labyrinth, believing I had failed to hear. Come to find out, I had failed to listen.

Just as I was about to leave the center of the labyrinth, a thought fell into my mind like a stone into water. Though the thought held substance and weight, all I could really see of it were the ripples it caused. It was more like listening to the echo of a voice than listening to the voice itself, or like noticing someone had already passed by and seeing only the person's back. The thought went something like this:

> First I tried to talk with you about your worries, and you chased me out of your mind. I tried to talk with you about your hopes and dreams, and again you chased me away. Finally, I tried to talk with you about those you love and those you've lost, and you wouldn't listen. I am in all these things and I am with you in all these things.

So I started the first circle again.

Practice: Journaling

Truth is, we don't always know what's important in our own minds. This week, let your mind wander wherever it wants, and write down what's going on in you. Frederick Buechner encourages, "Listen to your life."* Journaling provides a way to do that. By writing down the seemingly random thoughts, images, names, faces, and daydreams you come across, you'll have a place to return to them and pay closer attention. Is something coming up regularly that you hadn't noticed before? Why? Does a particular thought or name or image get your heart rate up? Why? As thoughts come to you and you begin to gain clarity, ask for wisdom and guidance to act where you need to or to wait if the time is not ripe for action.

---

* Frederick Buechner, *Listening to Your Life: Daily Meditations with Frederick Buechner* (New York: HarperCollins, 1992), 2.

May I learn to make good
out of what I'm given
Rather than only make sense of it.

May I be too engaged in
*   risking my own failures*
To have time to criticize the failures
*   of others.*

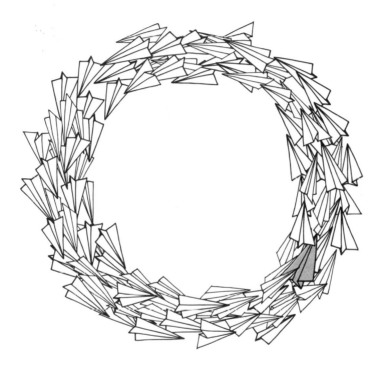

May I find freedom in limitation—
    to fully give myself
To what I can do
    rather than worry about what I
    cannot.

May I be the same
        in character and posture
Regardless of my circumstances.

May I be an uncompromisingly
        whole person.

May I have the eyes to see this
    as a good world in need of
    restoration
Rather than a bad world and
    an obstacle to my personal peace
    and rest.

Before I see someone as a problem,
may I see him or her as
a human being.

SACRED ANTACIDS

A young man came to his priest. "I feel like something is terribly wrong in my spirit. Please help me."

The priest replied, "Can you describe the feeling?"

"It happens every night," the young man said. "I lie down and begin thinking over my day, when a terrible feeling comes over me—a burning in my heart, like the burning the disciples felt when meeting Jesus on the road to Emmaus. But when I feel it, it feels like something is wrong. It's more like a pain. It's as if God is trying to tell me something. Please help me. What does it mean?"

The priest bent forward from his chair, reaching into his satchel. The young man, thinking the priest was climbing out of his chair to kneel on the ground and pray, slid out of his chair onto the floor, bowing his head and extending his hands, palms up, to receive the priest's blessing.

But instead of offering a prayer, the priest laid a single antacid in the young man's open hands. "You've got heartburn, son."

— — — — —

Don't get me wrong. I do regularly pray. And sometimes I'm praying about a physical discomfort.

But sometimes I just need an antacid,
and sometimes I just need to eat better,
and sometimes I need to sleep more,
and sometimes I need to see a professional therapist,
and sometimes I need to change the shoes I'm running in.

And I think all these things are spiritual matters.

In the past I might have suggested that therapy, exercise, and medicine were unspiritual things, as opposed to prayer, fasting, and meditation. Nowadays, I wonder if it is unspiritual to consider one aspect of my life spiritual, leaving all other aspects of myself partitioned off. I wonder if thinking spiritually means seeing my whole life (emotional, psychological, physiological, religious, economic, social, familial) as singular—as if my Creator is concerned with every inch and aspect of my whole self.

I don't believe it is at all unspiritual, much less un-Christian, to see a therapist or take an antacid. I do think, on the other hand, that it is distinctly un-Christian to separate the physical or financial parts of my life from my "spiritual life." God, whose greatest revelation of Himself was to become fully human, has great concern with all of me.

I find that one of the most powerful aspects of the Incarnation story is the thirty years of silence before the recorded part of Jesus's life. That silence—since nobody found much of it worth marking down—says to me that Jesus lived a life that was in large part unremarkable, until He was baptized by John. Many days I find my life to be somewhat unremarkable: I work, I eat, I rest, I have time with family and friends. Nothing out of the ordinary—not even a flash of celestial glory. I am encouraged that Jesus lived such a life as well, at least for a time.

Unlike many other ancient incarnation stories wherein a god takes on human form for a while and only to serve a special purpose, in Jesus, God not only became a human being, but He . . .

was carried in a woman's body,
was born to that woman,
was raised in a family with parents who taught Him to feed Himself, and had a dad.

And it seems, somewhere along the way, He . . .

lost His dad,
had siblings,
had friends,
lost friends,
lived in a neighborhood,
had neighbors,
held a job,
worked for money,
paid for food,
and paid taxes.

All of which says to me that these things are not insignificant in their normality but that God finds worth in spending most of a human lifetime attending to simple things like work and neighbors and friendships and family.

It seems that God not only abides mundane things but also dwells in them and does so gladly. And if that's true, which I believe it is, it means He dwells in me and my work and my community. A community of beautifully normal people with jobs and kids and mortgages and leaky faucets and disagreements and heartburn and issues to work though externally and interpersonally. A community that gathers on Sundays to celebrate and remember the One who is glorious and majestic and who was carried in the womb of a teenaged girl to be born into the world just as any of us normal folks were.

It means that everything matters.

Not just a world I cannot see, but the world right in front of me.

My job matters.
My bank account matters.
My education matters.
My health matters.

Practice: Exercise

This week, get your body involved in your prayer life. Maybe simply take a walk each day. Or maybe do something a bit more involved and intense. Regardless of what you choose, let that time be an intentional offering; pause before you get started and be conscious that God is present to you. If you walk, let your mind wander to whatever spaces of your life it wants to, and then ask for wisdom in each space. If you're in the gym, consider using the time between sets to contemplate something troubling or reflect on something for which you are thankful. Or consider letting that time be a respite from thoughts and images and anxieties and daydreams altogether. Perhaps listen to your footsteps or your own breathing.

There is often a clarity of mind that comes after exercise. Instead of quickly moving on to whatever is next on your agenda, capture that moment of clarity with a journal, notebook, or voice recorder. For the record, clarity won't always mean discerning a clear plan of action where you had none before; in fact, sometimes it will mean gaining clarity on your limitations and experiencing peace in relinquishing what is beyond your control.

If intentional prayer and reflection are distracting or difficult while you're exercising, consider using the gift of that clarity and peace after a workout to focus on a part of your life, a decision you need to make, or a specific relationship that is drawing your attention. Again, don't necessarily expect an answer, per se. You may not need an answer—you may need to see more clearly. You may need to see a situation or relationship more comprehensively. You may need vision. The clarity of mind that exercise offers can be a great tool in capturing vision.

*May I speak into the lives
of those I love
Because I love them and not because
I think I'm right.*

Even in conflict, may I see people
as beloved
Instead of problematic.

*May I have the vision to see this day
(and the work that comes with it)
as a gift.*

May my limitations be doorways
to partnership and relationship
Rather than reasons to feel shame
and isolation.

May I learn what it means
to have enough
And abandon the relentless pursuit
of "more."

*May love and forgiveness for others
be less and less optional.*

CHANGING TOILET PAPER

The cabbie was an older gentleman who eagerly and quickly engaged me in conversation. During our short talk, I mentioned that I would be married soon.

"Married?" he said. "So you love her, do you?"

"Yes sir. I sure do."

"Well, son." He paused, glancing at me in the rearview mirror. "You be sure to change that toilet paper before she asks."

I turned to gaze at the scenery as it streaked by the window. "You bet," I said, as if his comment made all the sense in the world. In reality, I couldn't figure out how he went so quickly from getting married and being in love to doing chores. What was *that* all about?

He seemed to pick up on my disconnect and said, "I'm serious, now. You gotta do it."

"All right," I assured him. "You got it." I hoped that would be the end of it. But it wasn't.

"Kid, you don't get it. I lost my marriage. I shoulda changed the toilet paper."

Looking up, I could see him staring at the road in front of us, shaking his head. "I'm telling you . . ." he said, talking to himself as much as to me. "I'm telling you, it would have made a difference."

He was right. I didn't get it. But I remembered that conversation and have been a regular toilet-paper changer throughout the course of my marriage. It turns out that being on toilet-paper duty is less about doing a simple chore and more about loving my wife. It has been about living in a posture of service. I've learned that the little things don't add up to a healthy relationship; they are symptomatic of it. Changing the toilet paper serves as a practice of sorts for my heart. It is a discipline, a habit, that roots me in a love that gives. I have to take time and energy away from something else in my day, something I would rather be doing, in order to change the toilet paper. And it would seem that doing so is a small thing because it takes only a few short minutes, even if the paper rolls are in another room of the house. But it's not the size of the job I face when I do it; it's my will. And if I am unable or unwilling to do such a small thing as this for my wife, it is less likely that I will serve her well when it actually costs me or inconveniences me.

So it is with prayer, sacrifice, or any spiritual practice. Take fasting, for instance. Skipping meals can seem only loosely associated with the practical, daily occurrences of life. But I have found that voluntarily and regularly removing a comfort from my life readies my heart to make more urgent, everyday sacrifices when they are called for.

When my neighbor's work schedule changes and her son needs a ride to school,
when my friends can't pay their rent or mortgage,
when war terrorizes a country, and those left behind need to rebuild,
when drought comes and hope seems to dry up with the land,
when the shaky ground of politics opens up and swallows whole families and cities and nations,
will I be practiced enough at the art of sacrifice to respond with courage, hope, and wisdom?

Prayer and fasting can seem divorced from normal life, but the posture I learn to live in, particularly as I voluntarily give up my own comforts, prepares me to give myself away when the time comes to do so.

Practice: Fasting

This week, choose something you regularly consume and give it up. For instance, consider skipping a meal or beverage and then doing two things with that sacrifice: First, use the time you'd normally spend preparing and consuming that favorite thing to reflect on your blessings and pray for those who lack the same. Second, keep track of the money you'd otherwise have spent on that favorite thing and, at the end of your fast, commit that money to providing for folks living without basic needs.

If skipping food or beverages doesn't work for you, maybe you watch television at night or listen to music or a podcast on the way to work. Consider turning that off this week and using that time to reflect on and pray for the relationships you've been given. Consider keeping a journal of your reflections and prayers. You just might be surprised to see whose faces and names come to mind when you give your heart room.

May I receive every good thing
as a gift
To be celebrated with thankfulness
and shared in generosity.

May my pursuit of happiness
never come at the cost
Of someone else's freedom
to do the same.

May I have enough faith
in the truth
That I happily abandon
the temptation to sell it.

May the depth of my generosity
never be swayed
By the depth of thanks I receive.

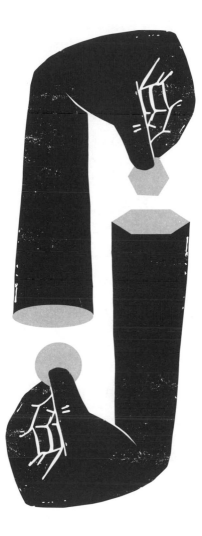

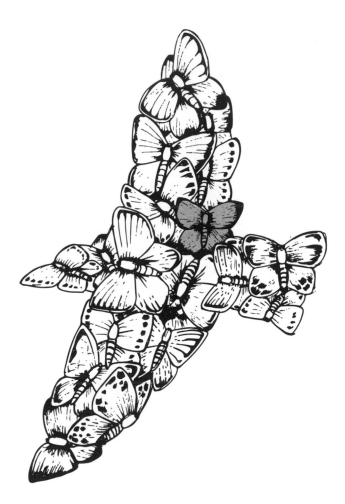

May I take joy in bearing witness
to great deeds and works
Without having to be
the source of them.

May my hope for others
never be darkened
By my personal disappointments.

SHELVING AND MINDFULNESS

A few months before the birth of our first child, my wife and I took a hurried survey of our small home and concluded that we did not have enough space. Creating space in our home mainly meant adding storage and, having run out of closet space, adding shelves. The thought of assembling shelves led me to a moment of humble recognition: I was going to need help. I have all the handyman prowess of the average toddler. So I called my friend Jesse, who agreed to swing by the following Saturday and help me set up a fitted wardrobe system from IKEA.

That Saturday, I had set aside a solid three hours for the project. But after only an hour of work, Jesse and I were finished. Which is to say that Jesse had finished with the actual building, and I had finished holding things he wasn't using while he worked.

Normally, I would have moved on from that completed project to something else needing attention. Between work-related items and those that come with being a husband and homeowner, I can always find something that needs doing. But on this particular Saturday afternoon, in a moment of something resembling wisdom, I gave myself a gift: I stopped. I sat there in front of this now-completed shelving unit and took in all that was happening around me—beginning with what was right in front of me.

There were new shelves in my home.
They were there because I have friends who joyfully and skillfully help me when I ask.
I needed Jesse's help with those shelves because I have a son on the way.
I have a son on the way.
I have a son on the way because I am married to this delightful

woman. This woman will be an inspiringly good mother.

I am going to be a father.

And even if our place is small, it is certainly enough.

And, if I'm honest, I know that I have always had enough.

This went on for close to an hour. And I realized that the whirlwind of gifts and delights I found swirling around my mind were always right there but that I had hardly ever slowed down enough, much less stopped, to see them and enjoy them. My anxieties pull me ever and always into the next moment, even before I've fully noticed the one I'm in. And in so doing, I worry because I don't know what will happen in that next moment, the next day, or next year. I've never known what tomorrow holds. But pausing there in that room, I knew for certain what the day had held and that it was one more day like so many that had passed without my noticing: a day in which I had enough.

Practice: Meditation

Make time this week to stop and pay attention. That might mean pausing to look over your own life and history. It might mean practicing mindfulness, recognizing what you have in the midst of a quiet moment. If you are like me, a more contemplative or meditative posture doesn't come naturally, so I've included a practice I've adopted and found exceedingly helpful. It's called Lectio Divina.

Following are the guidelines for this exercise, which can take twenty minutes to an hour.

1. Find a quiet, comfortable place to sit.
2. Choose a short passage from Scripture, such as Psalm 86:1–13.
3. Ask the Spirit to meet you and guide you.
4. Read the passage once to get familiar with it.
5. Reread the passage more slowly. Listen for a word or phrase that stands out and catches your attention and write that word or phrase down. It can help to read the passage softly out loud. You will often hear it in a different way by doing so.
6. Be quiet and listen. Then slowly repeat the word or phrase. Does it call to mind anything about your life or circumstances? If so, write that down too.
7. Read the whole passage again and pay attention to the way your word or phrase ties into it. You may discover another word or phrase that stands out to you. Write it down.
8. Read what you've written down. What life experiences come to mind? What thoughts or pictures or images come to mind? What person or specific situation? Remember that you are not alone; God is with you.
9. Read the whole passage slowly a fourth time. Again let your word or phrase be a starting point for your conversation with the Lord.
10. Tell God what you have noticed. Ask about what you don't understand. Ask what it is you are to do as a result of this time.

May I have the courage to
give my darker moments
a place in my process,
Knowing that they are only a part
and not definitive.

May the depth and energy
of my criticism
Be at least equaled by the depth
of my commitment to help.

May my disappointments
in myself and others
Lead me to hope for
and work for change
Rather than lead me to
distance myself.

May my awareness of faults
in myself or others
Never open the door to spite
but grant me a deep appreciation
for grace.

Prayer 27

*May I have hope for myself
the way I do for others.*

May I never grow tired
of starting over or
helping others do the same.
My hope is always in renewal and
resurrection.

THIS IS PRAYER TOO

The young man heaved himself down the center aisle toward the altar. He stopped every few steps to lean against one of the pew ends while the spins passed. The bottle in his hand felt hot, slippery; it wasn't the same bottle he started his day with, and it wasn't helping keep the taste of rage and regret out of his mouth.

He slowly made his way to the bottom step of the altar stairs. Standing still, he let the years of anger in his belly hold him to the ground like a millstone. He had seen this moment in his mind hours earlier and knew he needed to be right here . . . right where he was standing. He also knew he had to say something. At some point in the day, he'd planned it out, word for word. He might have even written it down . . . but on what? Where was that note? Where did he get the pen? He checked each jacket pocket and then scanned the room to see if anyone was watching. His eyes rested for a moment on the ornate reredos of John the Baptist and Mary, the mother of Jesus.

"How can you trust Him?" Silence.
"How can I trust You?" Silence.

Raising both his hands over his head, he brought the half-full bottle down to the ground in a brown crash of glass and booze. He steadied himself, waiting for the wave of nausea and tears to pass. His mouth moved over the words, but his voice couldn't catch them: "That's all I have for You."

Later that night, one of the young priests who lived in a room across from the chapel knelt on that altar stair and carefully cleaned the mess from the floor. He pinched each shard of brown glass between his fingers and dropped it into a paper bag. After wiping down the steps, he tossed the wet rag into a bucket and, crossing himself, said, "Amen."

Amen. So be it.

Surely. Truly.

As if all of what happened in this room that night had been a single prayer—from the moment that broken, grieving man walked through the doors, to the angry words he left ringing out in the air and architecture, to the hands of the brother himself and the rags he used to clean up the mess.

Truly. Surely. So be it. Amen.

Practice: Lament

Anger, sadness, and disappointment are not signs of a breakdown of faith nor a weakness in faith. Expressed as lament, they can be a necessary act of faith. The ability to communicate dark thoughts and negative emotions can be a sign that a relationship is strong and we aren't afraid that our feelings, heavy as they may be, will sink it.

This week, give yourself permission to make frustration, sadness, or anger part of your prayer life. If you've hit a really rough patch or you've been hurt, take some time to talk with God about it. Consider going on a walk where you can be alone, and say something like, "I can't believe this happened. I don't know what to do about it and I'm really lost." You might need to communicate frustration with God. He can take it. It can also be helpful to write out a bit of what you talk about.

The practice of lament can uncover wounds you haven't taken care of that need attention. Consider inviting someone else, perhaps even a professional, to help you process your thoughts and feelings. You are not designed to carry every weight on your own. Along with asking God to carry your burdens, consider that you may have good friends who are particularly equipped to help carry them as well.

May the urgency with which
I approach my work
Never become anxiety.
The world is not mine to save.

(*Inspired by Tyler Wigg-Stevenson*)

May my good works
    be fruits of my life
Rather than
    justification of it.

May I never consider
    my weaknesses and faults
The larger or most authentic
    part of me.

May I have the freedom to fail,
even at things I care about,
Knowing that mistakes aren't the end
of my process but part of it.

Though I know I am influenced
by my past,
May it never rule me
or define who I am entirely.

May it be enough for me
to see God in the world.

THE TRAVELER'S NEEDS

A traveler and his companion prepared to set out on a long journey. In preparation, the traveler packed a second coat.

His companion asked, "Why are you bringing a second coat?"

The traveler responded, "I will need it."

The traveler then packed a second pair of shoes.

His companion asked, "Why are you bringing a second pair of shoes?"

The traveler responded, "I will need them."

The traveler then packed extra food into his bag. Two of every kind of food he would bring.

His companion asked, "Why are you bringing two of every kind of food?"

The traveler responded, "I will need it."

The traveler's companion finally set his small bag down and said, "Look how heavy your load is. Mine is light. I have but one coat, one pair of shoes, and just enough food for the days we will be walking. Why do you need so much?"

The traveler said, "Because your coat is old and thin, and your shoes are old and worn. Having walked with you, I also know that you grow hungry often."

Confounded, the companion said, "But when I asked you about

these things, you told me you would need them, not that *I* would need them."

"You are my companion," said the traveler. "So long as we walk together, there is no difference between your needs and mine."

Practice: Intercession

Spend some time this week thinking about, remembering, and praying for the people your own provision serves—the people who benefit from the gifts and strengths you are given. Consider making a written list of those closest to you and then wait to see what other names or faces come to mind. You may be surprised at whose faces and names those are. In some cases, you may have a strong sense of what others need. At times, the people who come to mind are in situations well beyond your wisdom or reach. In those cases, it can be enough to simply remember those people and their situations. Consider praying something as simple as "Lord, have mercy" or maybe not using any words at all. To remember others in silence as they face trials and difficulties is a form of intercession.

Also, consider letting a few of those folks know they came to mind. Again, you may be surprised at what happens in the hearts, minds, neighborhoods, and general lives of those you remember and pray for.

May the reality that
    I cannot know the whole truth
Give me freedom to talk
    about the part I can see
    rather than paralyze me.

May I love those less fortunate
than I am,
As well as those
who have had great success.
Free me from the burden of envy.

May I have the courage
*   to expect good for my life*
*   and world,*
And resilience if and when
those expectations are disappointed.

May my value for this world
and the people in it
Extend far beyond the uses
I have for them.

May I believe
that newness is possible.

IT WILL PASS

The young woman sat in a wooden chair across from her mentor and grieved, "I am so easily distracted. My mind buzzes with noise and I cannot pray. Please help me."

Her mentor nodded slowly and smiled, saying, "It will pass. Keep practicing."

One week later, the young woman sat across from her mentor again. This time, sliding slightly lower into the chair, she stared at the empty table. "Nothing works. I sit in silence. I journal. I read the Scriptures. Still, my mind is too noisy. I cannot pray. Please help me."

Her mentor nodded slowly and smiled, saying, "It will pass. Keep practicing."

Many weeks went by, during which the young woman did not visit her mentor—until one day, she bounded into the room and stood at the table, beaming. "You were right! I kept practicing. I sat in silence. I journaled. I read the Scriptures. And eventually the busyness of my mind settled like dust and I could pray! I can pray!"

Her mentor rose from the table, set her hand on the young woman's shoulder, and smiled. "It will pass," she said. "Keep practicing."

May I grow in love and in GOD and those

wisdom and in
favor with
I am given to.

— — **Scott would like to thank:**

Holly, Anders, Elsa, Jones for being my beloved tribe.

Justin McRoberts for being a tremendous co-conspirator.

Joy Eggerichs Reed for fighting the good fight.

Morris Dirks for giving me a place to be poor in spirit.

Chris Carson, Scott Calgaro, Carly Taylor, Vince Buriens, and the whole Jubilee family for helping us birth this project.

Caitlin Beidler for unrelenting belief in my work.

All my friends. You know who you are and how you've helped. I love you.

Ecclesia Houston, Imago Dei Community, Union Chapel, Church on Morgan, and Cascade Church for all letting me be artsy-fartsy within their community.

— — **Justin would like to thank:**

Amy, Asa and Katelyn for sharing in this with me so generously.

Scott Erickson for being a stupendous co-laborer.

Joy Eggerichs Reed for kindly and thoughtfully helping me navigate new waters.

Chris Carson, Scott Calgaro, Carly Taylor, and Vince Buriens for creating a culture that challenges me to see that part of what makes tomorrow better is the work I put into it.

Byron Borger for believing in books and in the women and men who write them.

Shelter-Vineyard Church and the Church Without Shoes family for being exactly that: Family.

Donna Hatasaki and The Good Way.

Suzie Johnson, Keith Bordeaux, Keely Scott, and Compassion International for giving me the chance to see what prayer looks like in the hearts and lives of children.

ABOUT THE AUTHORS

Justin McRoberts is a songwriter, author, speaker, and retreat leader. He lives in the East San Francisco Bay area with his wife, son, and daughter.

justinmcroberts.com

 @justinmcroberts

Scott Erickson is a working studio artist, author, and storyteller. He lives in Portland, Oregon, with his wife and three children.

scottericksonart.com

 @scottthepainter

Both Justin and Scott travel regularly to perform and teach.